PRAISE FOR *POEMS FOR THE PEOPLE*

Nicole Tallman's *Poems for the People* is a gorgeous and tender love song for all of us—the grievers, the poets, the stricken and the soft. Tallman's poems highlight the beauty and heartbreak we live through, but also examine and expand what it means to truly relate with others, to know us in a way that only a friend can: by holding us together in her esteem.

--- JARED BELOFF,
   AUTHOR OF *WHO WILL CRADLE YOUR HEAD*

These poems especially excel at one of my favorite things poems can do—they open up a dialogue, they start a conversation. And, like a good conversationalist, they ask you questions, they tell you about themselves, they braid together the languages of the philosophical, surprise, and the quotidian. They look you in the eye and ask you how you feel. They're poems for The Astro Poets and soft boys, for Sylvia Plath and people who say they don't pray. For poets and lovers of poetry and people who don't like poems. They're poems for Nicole herself and also for you. Poems for all of us. What a gift.

--- AARON BURCH,
   AUTHOR OF *YEAR OF THE BUFFALO*

In this ambitious yet graceful collection, Nicole Tallman is quick to tell (nay, show) us what she is about. Uncommonly confident, Tallman asks what happens when we "wade out way too far" while in the same breath lauding the "plain talk" of poems, the girls she "wanted to hug a little too long." Written with a deft hand, these elegiac and tender poems promise "permanent day or never-ending night." Buy this book, support this impressive outing: "where I come from, it's also about the merchandise."

--- MICHAEL CHANG,
   AUTHOR OF *BOYFRIEND PERSPECTIVE & ALMANAC*
   OF USELESS TALENTS

Nicole Tallman is a poet looking for the truth.

--- ALEX DIMITROV,
   AUTHOR OF *LOVE AND OTHER POEMS*

Nicole Tallman writes poems for everyone and to everything. Her clear and concise diction in *Poems for the People* can be both comforting and cutting (sometimes within the same poem). This deft balance permits the poems to honestly explore topics as wide ranging as love, family and death, to witches, fast food and pop culture, and all without sacrificing their emotional power. Often in language, what is put most plainly is closest to the truth, and Tallman's poetics play within the logics of this axiom, conjuring a surplus of meaning through enchantments of common speech. The poet and lover of poetry will certainly find much to admire in this book, but *Poems for the People* is (as the title suggests) for all people; so a special warning to those who claim to be resistant to the power of poetry: beware! Given over to the spells of Tallman's lyricism, incisive wit and capacious spirit, you may find yourself not only reading her poetry, but praying along with it.

--- **ADRIAN DALLAS FRANDLE**

I love these poems. I love that they are clear and generous gifts for real people, even while Tallman is creating art in her own wild, unique, and powerful way—a way, thankfully, that never excludes the people, the reader, that ultra-private curious audience of one who will pick up this book and find a poem that has been written just for them. P.S. On a personal note, future readers, I found myself in many many of these poems, but the one that seemed written just for me is "Poem for the Introverts." Which one did she write for you?

--- **MAUREEN SEATON,**
    AUTHOR OF *UNDERSEA*

Not bad.

--- **DALE TALLMAN,**
    NICOLE TALLMAN'S DAD

POEMS FOR THE PEOPLE

POEMS FOR THE PEOPLE

by Nicole Tallman

Southern Collective Experience

www.southerncollectiveexperience.com

Copyright © 2023 by Nicole Tallman

All rights reserved. No part of this book may be reproduced or transmitted in any form or by any means, electronic or mechanical, including photocopying, recording, or any information storage and retrieval system, without permission in writing from the publisher.

ISBN: 978-1-7362306-2-6

Printed in the United States of America

This paper meets the requirements of ANSI/NISO Z39.48-1992 (Permanence of Paper)

Cover Design and formatting by Kaitlyn Young

For the people

I don't know whose side you're on, but I am here for the people...
—Jericho Brown

CONTENTS

POEM FOR THE DEAD (INCLUDING MY MOM).....1
POEM FOR THE GRIEVING.....2
POEM FOR TOO DARK.....3
POEM FOR SYLVIA PLATH.....4
POEM FOR THE SUICIDAL.....8
POEM FOR THE WITCHES.....9
POEM FOR MY HYSTER SISTERS.....10
POEM FOR PERIMENOPAUSAL WOMEN.....21
POEM FOR PEOPLE WHO
DON'T LIKE POEMS (INCLUDING MY DAD).....22
POEM FOR PEOPLE WHO
DON'T LIKE CANDY CORN (INCLUDING A.C.).....23
POEM FOR THE ASTRO POETS.....24
POEM FOR THE SOFT BOYS.....25
POEM FOR PEOPLE WHO ARE TIRED.....27
POEM FOR PEOPLE WHO TAKE PUBLIC TRANSIT.....28
POEM FOR PEOPLE WHO
HAVE WORKED THE FAST FOOD COUNTER.....29
POEM FOR THE GUY IN THE ELEVATOR.....31
POEM FOR 17 MUTUALS.....33
POEM FOR THE JURORS.....34
POEM FOR MY FRIEND K.....35
POEM FOR GENERATION X.....36
POEM FOR PEOPLE WHO
DON'T LIKE THE BEACH WHEN IT'S SUNNY.....37
POEM FOR THE MIDWEST GOTHS.....38
POEM FOR THE HEATHENS.....39
POEM FOR PEOPLE WHO SAY THEY DON'T PRAY.....40
POEM FOR THE MOONLOVERS.....41
POEM FOR LONGTERM LOVERS.....42
POEM FOR ONLY CHILDREN.....43
POEM FOR THE PHOBICS.....44
POEM FOR THE "DISORDERED" EATERS.....45
POEM FOR THE LOVESICK.....46
POEM FOR THE INTROVERTS.....47
POEM FOR PEOPLE WITH A PHONE IN THEIR HAND.....48
POEM FOR THE LIVING.....49

NOTES.....51
ACKNOWLEDGMENTS.....53

POEM FOR THE DEAD (INCLUDING MY MOM)

Since we'll likely never be together again
anywhere but here—what season
were you most alive in?
Is there morning or color where you are?
Do you have freedom? If so, how are you using it?
Would you rather be a bird or an angel?
Permanent day or never-ending night?
If there are hours, when are your most difficult?
Do you know who you were
before this? Why or why not?
And now that there's fire —
are you in Heaven or Hell?
More time or less?
Do you still feel happiness?
Would you return?
To Earth, this dream, or anywhere else?

POEM FOR THE GRIEVING

The summer sky opens up orange.

Text around circle (starting from top, clockwise): ...how many bodies have gone down to be reborn? Water too cold to swim in, we all wade out way too far. A single swan ignoring the warning; a shiver as the summer shifts to fall. Yawning the boy goes to catch morning, my father walks the wet cemetery alone. Days and days of no rain, he drags a jug heavy with sorrow. My mother is buried too. Face. There are no flowers left to water. Green rocks long becoming the color. There is no redemption here; only rest, seeing my face reflect off the gray of the day; the stillness of all who have touched the bottom before me—

POEM FOR TOO DARK

Who are you?	ONE FROM YOUR PAST
What is your name?	TOO DARK
Are you a good spirit?	NO
Do you want to harm me?	NO
What do you want me to know?	UNCLEAR
What is my purpose in this life?	FUTURE HAZY
Are you ok?	NO
Can I help?	NO
Can I speak to Sylvia Plath?	NO
Can I speak to my mother?	YES
How do I talk to her?	ASK
When will I die?	SUMMER
How will I die?	LEAVE ME NOW

POEM FOR SYLVIA PLATH

TOO DARK told me I couldn't speak to you through my Ouija Board, so I'm going to try to reach you through this poem. I want you to know how famous you are now and how many people adore you. My favorite poem of yours is "Tulips" and I also really love "Edge," which is credited as the last known poem you wrote, but that's debatable because Ted burned your last journal. That's also debatable.

I also want you to know that there's a 1,154-page biography about you called *Red Comet* and that your tarot deck recently sold on Sotheby's for $200,000. Can you believe that? Can you believe that some of your fans take a trip to Indiana just to see your braid? Others go to your grave in Heptonstall to deface the Hughes name from your headstone.

You also have a bot that is quite active on Twitter. You probably don't know what that means, but I think you may have liked Twitter and would have had a lot of followers. Ok, you probably wouldn't have liked Twitter, but you definitely would have had a lot of followers. I would have loved to follow you.

I follow Frieda for you on Instagram. You probably don't know what that means either, but it's a place where she posts photos of a menagerie of pets (including 14 owls!), paintings, cooking, nature walks, motorbikes, and flowers. I learned from Instagram that she had a big art exhibit in London recently.

POEM FOR THE SUICIDAL

A winter wish for the taste
of snow in my mouth—
pill or real, does it matter?

The way the grey stills us all.
I have been blue in my tired for so long.
Iris, let my rest come to me—

deep and violet.
No, it doesn't matter.
Let it come in fragments.

Let it come.
Angels dust my eyes with their white,
white, wings.

They aren't ready for us there yet.
There's so much left here
we haven't even seen.

POEM FOR THE WITCHES

I'm that cat in *Constantine*,
but I'm also human and I'm talking,
casting a love spell with broken violins.

Crystal, smoke, stone—
I'm a mystic, a sage, a good witch,
a lucky 13 wearing a white gown.

Isn't a wish a spell?
I say: Lift the world's sadness.
I chant: Oṃ maṇi padme hūṃ.

Isn't a prayer a kind of magic?
Isn't silence?
Isn't the moon?

POEM FOR MY HYSTER SISTERS

What they don't tell you before the hysterectomy

                                                is that most of your want may wane

    &   that you may awake to feel that you've been de-sexed

    &   that a uterus pulled through a vagina is a sedated form of birth

    &   you may walk cautiously for quite some time afterwards

    &   your bladder may often betray you

&   you may fear your own body and its lack of response to stimulation

&   if you save one ovary so you aren't forced into a violent menopause at the age of 37, you will still have a ghost period that can be spookier than a bloody one because you can't see it, which may make you feel like you're going crazy

&   other women will say you're so lucky to no longer bleed, but you will say that your one remaining ovary has jumped into overdrive—so much so that you may feel the acceleration of age, which may make you feel like you're turning 50 instead of 40

&   you can't take hormones to counter these side effects due to your predisposition to cancer so you will have to suffer through it, just like you suffered through the heavy, painful periods that prompted this surgery in the first place

&   you may feel very disconnected from your body in ways that mimic a depression, but people will ask how you can possibly feel depressed when your life is so amazing, and you will question your decision when hot flashes and brain fog further dismantle you

    &   you will ask if there is ever any real relief from being a woman.

POEM FOR PERIMENOPAUSAL WOMEN

I'm like a birch tree in the naked white of winter.
The birch that autocorrect first changed to *bitch* then *butch*.

I'm shedding layers of black and white paper and ash.
Newspapers have never been more alive or dead,

as I silence my phone and turn to
phonographs, still photography, and vinyl.

Here I find comfort,
among the old, the dusty, the musty, and familiar—the 1880s

and the 1980s
the granny panties and overwhelming old French perfumes.

Here I crank up the heady rose,
the saccharine violet, the languid linden blossom,

resurrect the pink fluorescent
of my faded Electric Youth.

POEM FOR PEOPLE WHO DON'T LIKE POEMS (INCLUDING MY DAD)

So, I wrote this poem for your acceptance.
Someone told me I shouldn't admit that.
Someone also once told me not to use the word poem in a poem.
Well, poem, poem, poem.
I'm going to use this poem to break the stupid rules.
I'm also going to write plainly so everyone can see it.
Ready?
This is a poem.
My dad says he's a simple man and doesn't understand poems.
I'm going to write so he can understand this poem.
He likes plain talk.
He probably still won't like this poem.
And likely neither will you.
But I'm still going to write it.
And if you're the only person who likes this poem, I've made a big difference.
This is a poem, and I hope it's no longer for you.

POEM FOR PEOPLE WHO DON'T LIKE CANDY CORN (INCLUDING A.C.)

Adrian says candy corn is not really candy.
I say have you tried the chocolate variety?
How about the pumpkins?
He says gross.
We do an office poll: Top 10 Halloween Candy.
I ask if wax fangs are on the list.
They are not.
They should be.
Loren says it's Snickers, Snickers, Reese's, Snickers, Snickers.
I say Snickers are year-round candy.
I give Reese's a pass for the orange wrapper and wicked shapes variety.
Rachel loves Reese's. She says ha ha.
Leah says Milky Way and Twix.
I say that's definitely year-round candy.
Kisha says Halloween candy is anything gummy.
I agree, but think shape may matter—like maybe worms count, but not bears.
I say I love candy corn.
Others are appalled.
Andrea says I'm chaos.
I say I will dress like a giant candy corn for the office Halloween party.
I won't really do this.
I say I will write a poem about candy corn and dedicate it to Adrian.
This I do.
I write it.
This is that poem.
Do you like it?
Adrian loves it.
Says it's the only thing good about candy corn.
He prints it and pins it on his cubicle wall—right above his giant Reese's Easter Bunny.

POEM FOR THE ASTRO POETS

The Astro Poets say I'm a ?
because just like a Cancer
a ? looks you in the eye & asks how you feel.

Yes, I do that.
Way too often I've been told by some.
Sorry about that.

Why can't I be an ! like an Aries
& say everything
with conviction and passion?

Yes, I just asked another question.
Because I'm leaving everything open to input.
So Cancerian of me.

Well, at least my moon sign is a Virgo
& that means I'm also an open & lively (
but also care about everyone. :'(

Let's go to my rising sign:
Taurus. No, it's not even a full :
It's a ;

The full : would be a Leo,
who is always happy to make an entrance.
Yes, I am definitely @ <3 a Cancer.

& I borrowed all the .s in this poem from the Scorpios.
They are magnetic. But not magnetic enough to be the ...
Which sign do you think that is?

POEM FOR THE SOFT BOYS

Where I come from, there's a season for guns, as if rifles should be celebrated like Christmas.

There's a smell. I'd like to call it November, but it's a special blend of blood, rust, estrus, and a winter so cold it freezes the hair inside my nose.

There's a ritual. It's men dressed in camouflage and hunter orange. It's the law. And they stay out late on the 40 and chug 40s, perch up in trees or shelter in blinds, chew tobacco and build big fires.

Where I come from, it's also about the merchandise. The "Nice Rack" shirts and mounted deer heads on the wall. Not surprisingly, racks are one reason men prize the buck more than the doe.

There's a sound out my window where I come from. It's earsplitting gunfire and the fight between my uncle and cousin who never speak again.

There's a name for the soft boys where I come from, the ones who don't drive big trucks and don't refer to women as broads you just load up and throw in the back.

Where I come from, hunting is a blood sport. And it breeds blood-thirsty boys who think it's ok to say: Do what I say or I'll shoot you.

There's also a mascot: a dead deer, purple gray tongue out, gutted and hanging from the rafters of the garage. The same purple gray of the deer liver my dad left on the counter for my mom to cook.

She said it reminded her of afterbirth and made her gag.

POEM FOR PEOPLE WHO ARE TIRED

Today was a long day and I'm tired.
I'm just trying to write a poem after working 18 hours.
During a pandemic.
And after a night of little sleep.
Someone once told me not to mention being tired—
especially not at work.
I guess it makes us look lazy or unmotivated
or unprofessional. I don't know.
I think it's human to be tired.
How can we not be tired in 2023?
2020 barely started and never ended.
I'm just here to tell the truth.
Isn't that what poets are supposed to do?
Are you as tired as I am?
I'm tired of pretending not to be tired.
And of people not telling the truth.

POEM FOR PEOPLE WHO TAKE PUBLIC TRANSIT

I once tumbled down two entire flights of stairs while exiting a Metromover station in Miami and no one offered to help me up. Before boarding the train today, however, the automated announcer warns me to stand back from the platform. On the train, I must stay clear of the doors, she says. Not because she cares, but because departure is being delayed. For my safety, she tells me to hold the handrails. That doesn't feel safe during COVID, and the hand-sanitizer dispenser is empty. A sign says if I feel unsafe onboard, I can call 375-2700. Who can I call if I feel unsafe once I exit?

POEM FOR PEOPLE WHO HAVE WORKED THE FAST FOOD COUNTER

I worked at McDonald's one summer in high school, but only because my mother made me. The manager looked me up and down on day one and said, *No back kitchen for you. You're too pretty.* Sent me straight to the front counter. I should have quit on the spot, but I didn't.

Put on a purple shirt the color of Grimace and an ugly matching visor. Sold those burgers and super-size fries to even creepier guys than him. Burned my arm badly on the fry cooker and went home smelling like salt and grease.

Worked with a guy who rode his bicycle to and from work in a blizzard. He defended me when the customers got too aggressive over not having enough mustard or pickles. He also took the food the manager said to throw away home every night to his kids.

He said we were blessed to have a job.

POEM FOR THE GUY IN THE ELEVATOR

A guy in the elevator at work turned to me and said: *It's all too much. Don't you feel like we're all just waking up and going through the motions?* I didn't say what I wanted to because I never know who is listening. I just looked at him and said: *I hope it gets better soon.*

Maybe I should have said more. Maybe I should have asked if he was ok, even though I already knew the answer. He looked intense, yet defeated. Have you ever seen a one-winged bird fighting for a crust of bread? I have. But I'd never seen that guy in the elevator before.

He was wearing all black in the middle of a heat wave. I often do the same. As if wearing all black places us closer to death. As if buying another leather jacket in the summer makes any sense. Do we want to live to see another summer?

That's what I wanted to say.

POEM FOR 17 MUTUALS

I swallowed a pill; I swallowed a pine cone.
The world ends like an almond tree pulled by its roots.
I don't want to drive my car into that tree anymore.

Cold spot near mom's favorite recliner,
I've nothing to offer but
that deer there, cracked at the spine, oozing onto roadside rock.

My days are numbered, just like yours.
I flinch at each number like a gun has gone off.
I'll be dead soon enough—

cradled above the earth, rocked gently to sleep
to a primal white sky, wheeling on.
I worried there'd be nothing more than a silver vortex.

In places like this, I am a ghost,
a serpent that rattles against silent stone floors,
in a room with glimpses of yesterday, displayed along alabaster walls.

Once I watched a boy disappear under the surface a lake.
Some words are too big to mean anything.
I'm saving the story for the afterlife.

There's no need to close the door on your way out.

POEM FOR THE JURORS

Grab a clip and have a seat inside.
You should never underestimate your value.
This is a duty, not a privilege.
One of the most patriotic expressions of citizenship.
There is no justice without you.
With great power comes great responsibility.
Your job is to determine the truth.
Your decision will affect a stranger's life.
And the lives of the people who love that person.
There is no justice without you.
You can watch a movie while waiting for your number to be called.
The bathrooms are to the left and the lunchroom is to the right.
You will be reimbursed $15 for the day.
Yes, for the entire day.

POEM FOR MY FRIEND K

Yesterday, my friend K told me the story of how she keeps her dead cat in the freezer next to her mother's dead puppy. She stores him in a garbage bag between a jumbo bag of pot-stickers and margarita mix. The cat is black, in case you're wondering. I know because I asked. I also asked why she didn't bury them both in the backyard. She said she said there simply wasn't space. The cat died young. She suspected it was parvo contracted from her mother's new puppy. I had to Google parvo, which I learned is short for parvovirus—a highly contagious disease often spread by direct contact with infected blood, feces, urine or other bodily fluids. I didn't ask the cat's name. I should have. Would it be weird to bring it up again now? Should I just text her: What's the name of the dead cat you keep in the freezer? I guess I could. I mean, she did seem ok talking about it. I think enough time has passed. She also told me how her estranged father was semi-famous for suing a police officer for stealing his severed leg. Then she told me how she can't seem to keep a boyfriend or a girlfriend for long, which is surprising because she has a lot of great stories.

POEM FOR GENERATION X

Dear Topps Company:

I would like you to know that I grew into my Garbage Pail Kids name.

And that, in case of a fire, my GPK collection is one of the few things I plan to take with me.

And when I evacuated for Hurricane Irma, I grabbed 6 material possessions:

- my purse
- my photo album
- my first teddy bear
- a safe with important documents
- my deceased mother's jewelry
- and my collection of GPK cards.

I would like R.L. Stine (aka R.L. Slime) to know that I'm no middle-grader, but I got goosebumps when I cracked open *Welcome to Smellville*.

It's now on my bookshelf—displayed prominently—among my not-so-juvenile (and not-so-gross) poetry books.

I guess you could say I'm still an '80s kid, and I'm nostalgic for the '80s.

I would also like you to know that I own the GPK movie and the cartoon series.

And that, at the height of the pandemic, I tried to dig them out of storage to re-watch them.

They were under too many heavy boxes to get to, and I was tired, so I settled for my new GPK book and stickers.

It was good to see my old friends Adam Bomb, Babbling Brooke, Brainy Janey, Cranky Frankie, Handy Sandy, Junkfood John, Luke Puke, Nervous Rex, Rob Slob and Wacky Jackie.

Thank you for the trip down memory lane and for some new GPK goods to look forward to.

Yours Truly,

Nutty Nicole

POEM FOR PEOPLE WHO DON'T LIKE THE BEACH WHEN IT'S SUNNY

Find me on Miami Beach in March when it's cloudy, wearing an Adidas tracksuit because a bikini is too much pressure, even if I still have the body for it—sort of. That's partially why I exist on espresso, fruit, yogurt, and yoga.

When the sun's too fierce, you can find me hiding under an umbrella, slathered in sunscreen because cancer, and aging, and all the other things I must defend against that prevent me from just enjoying the moment.

When it's overcast, I'll still be sporting sunglasses. I'll be ignoring the sand scraping between my toes. I'll be trying to tune out the Reggaeton. I'll be going to my happy place – a dark forest by the lake. A light November rain. I'll be warmed by winter wool, a wood-burning fire, a glass of wine.

POEM FOR THE MIDWEST GOTHS

I grew up in the middle of a cornfield, went to college in the middle of a cornfield. The smell of manure would wake me some mornings. I can remember my grandfather tossing me like a sack of old potatoes into the corn grinder for fun. I remember thinking I would lose a limb or two, before being ground to cornmeal. I remember cleaning the horse stables. Gagging in the hay. I remember picking sweet and sour berries, thorns tearing at my tender fingers. And later picking seeds out of my teeth after eating too many blackberries. The sun so hot shining down. I can still smell the dust and dirt—the change in the air and the rain from summer to fall. I remember fall in the haunted cornfield. Flannel. Black nails. Ghost stories. Reapers. Mazes. Hunts for crop circles and witches. Reading a Book of Shadows. Playing Light as a Feather, Stiff as a Board. Us heathens, summoning Candyman and Bloody Mary, in and out of mirrors. Taking swigs from a shared bottle of Boone's Farm. A fire, always a big fire, to soften the October blow. Someone telling a story of someone who died young among the corn. Who told the story, and who died young—that, I can't remember.

POEM FOR THE HEATHENS

I grew up without a church, borrowed a pew at a friend's in the summer. Drank the cloying fruit punch they served out of too-small paper cups. Ate their off-brand cookies. It was often dark and cool—the only light coming through the stained-glass windows. Light fractured like a prism. I stood at the feet of the crucified Jesus. Felt the puncture of nails and thorns. Put the dollar my mother gave me in the gold offering bowl. Everyone always seemed sad and solemn. I don't remember joy, but restraint. The smell of wax and bleach. The organ droning on. The few people who weren't tone deaf leading the chorus. My mind always wandering somewhere, anywhere, but there. To running outside in the grass. To playing Monkey in the Middle. To coloring. To Lazarus. To Gabriel. To Mary. To sin and suffering. To blood. To the priest in his simple robes. To the little green Bible he gave me. To his unwavering belief that he could actually save me. To the girls I wanted to hug a little too long.

POEM FOR PEOPLE WHO SAY THEY DON'T PRAY

This is a poem for people who say they don't pray.
Poem is a prayer.
If you write, you pray.
I write to the light of the candle.
I walk with the moon at the end of the day.
Walking is a prayer.
I write with the devotion of a nun to her god.
I walk with the devotion of a monk to his vow.
I repeat: anaphora.
I chant: *Oṃ maṇi padme hūṃ.*
I say: *Santa María, Madre de Dios.*
I write.
I walk.
I pray.
I burn incense for you.
Frankincense. Violet. Rose. Myrrh.
I pray.
I drink wine.
Prisoner Red Zin and Rombauer Chardonnay.
I pray.
I write.
I walk.
I say your name.
You don't answer.
I write.
I walk.
I drink.
I burn.
I chant.
I pray.

POEM FOR THE MOONLOVERS

Moon light over noon light
I dust hyperbole
I float on a lily-livered lie
If the center shifts ragged
I swim backstroke to shore
Sing to ruby-throated robins
Bow to pink-fingered roses freesia
Heal the wounded wasps dying in the hive

POEM FOR LONGTERM LOVERS

An avocado toast,
a bottle of Prosecco,
a sunlit balcony with fuchsia flowers,
a discussion of how everything grows old with time.

You say what's new isn't always better.
I speak of my old Mustang,
of our old relationship,
of the fatigue of years made older by a pandemic,

and I renew my commitment to what's lasting—
to your hands on my back, in my hair, when I'm stressed,
to when I feel like I can't go on any longer and you say,
Don't you know how amazing you are?

POEM FOR ONLY CHILDREN

I know why you're never and always lonely.

POEM FOR THE PHOBICS

Hippophobia sounds like the fear of the hippopotamus, but is really an alternate name for equinophobia, which is the fear of horses, which I have, to a degree (they need to keep their distance), but mostly because my mother told me a story at a young age of how a girl broke her pelvis after being thrown from a horse that went crazy, which I now realize is similar to a story she told me about a girl who broke her neck snow skiing and another girl who broke her back water skiing, and there are so many of these stories in my head about girls getting hurt that it's no wonder I have so much fear of what's larger than me, of things breaking, of behavior I can't quite control.

POEM FOR THE "DISORDERED" EATERS

A friend makes fun of me for eating the same breakfast every day: a cup of fat-free yogurt with 6 blueberries, 6 raspberries, a tsp of chia seeds & a tbs of oats. I'm always hungry two hours later.

We laugh at this & at how I'm either starving or stuffed. Feeling hangry or heavy. I don't seem to understand moderation. I eat no tacos or two too many.

A colleague tells me I'm too skinny, while another says I look *healthy*. So, am I a waif on a ledge or a cow on a prairie? I don't really care how either of them sees me. I'm too busy counting berries.

POEM FOR THE LOVESICK

I never would have left here sane. You had to drag me out mad. But driven out hard across the city, frostbitten ears and a mouth full of crumbs, I called all the doctors, and none would see me. When F said, *Let's just be friends*, I thought of all the bad reasons I had left home to come here. French and want. Nostalgia and desire. Dreams and dreams.

I didn't dream of this cold, of all my money going to taxes and rent, eating the same sandwich every day, or my pills running out. I didn't dream of F lying, or of the morning light pouring through my only window, staining everything a fungal green. I called my mother. *Please come get me*, I said. She had never wanted me to leave.

My mother who didn't like to travel or big cities rented a U-Haul. Drove alone all the way from Michigan to Montreal to help me clean up my folie. I cried all the way home. I want to go back, I said. She took my hand, and said, *No, you don't*. I slept in my childhood bed, healing my brain, for the next 2 of the bluest months. Changing my dreams back to English from French.

POEM FOR THE INTROVERTS

What's your spirit animal? The one you really relate to, not the one you tell people you are when asked in a professional setting. Like the time I told an interviewer I was a cheetah because I'm fast (sort of) and resourceful (definitely), when I really wanted to say I'm a snowy owl because I like to appear when I want to, limit human interaction, and I like the winter. But that's not something you say in an interview in Miami. I mean, unless you don't want the job. And I did want it (at the time) and did get it, in case you're wondering. Well, the snowy owl is my true spirit animal, and I'm saying it now and going forward. I could be happy alone for hours, or just chilling as the mascot for some library, or hanging out with Harry Potter and all the other introverts who really just want to remain magically mysterious.

POEM FOR THE PEOPLE WITH A PHONE IN THEIR HAND

I'm sitting at Hyam Plutzik's desk,
in the same chair that 1,000 famous(ish)
writers have sat in over the past 10
years, and I wonder if the wood could
serve as a board that summons the living
and the dead. Maybe then I could write
a truly great poem. One that gets published
in *The New Yorker,* which is all anyone seems
to care about anyway. I ask those who have sat
at this desk, in this exact same chair, to help me
out—just like I have asked Sylvia Plath. But she
simply told me to stop asking her for help and to start
writing. Her voice all clipped vowels and the confidence
of the dead. She'd grown tired of my excuses. Hyam,
hearing me now for the first time, is also telling me
to just pick up the pen. *Does anyone write by hand
anymore?* I ask him. He tells me to stop being
flippant. Look, I tell him, I'm typing this poem
on the phone in my hand. (A pencil and pad might make
a better planchette, but this phone is what I have.) Isn't it
sad that we always have our phones in our hands? I sort
of think so. I don't think we really know what to do anymore
unless there's a phone in our hands. I suppose I should
leave this room—put down my phone, go to the beach
or the pool. Maybe interact with other guests. But why
would I leave when all that I need to write is here
in this room—right in the palm of my hand?

POEM FOR THE LIVING

I love Miami in the winter.
I love Michigan in the fall.

I love the smell of the oldest books.
I love the smell of petrichor.

I love buying myself red roses.
I love building a fire in the snow.

I love Chartreuse, Champagne, and Chambord.
I love the way that sounds.

I love deep conversations with people I'll never see again.
I love the moon more than the sun.

I love Medusa and her head of snakes.
I love drawing the Hermit card.

I love being alone in the forest.
I love being alone in a field of lavender.

I love being alone without feeling lonely.
I love being an only child.

I love that happy hour isn't always happy.
I love not owning a home.

I love the seagull I once saw eating a discarded orange.
I love going to the beach when there's no sun.

I love when the muses speak to me.
I love the highest note on the violin.

I love the French who don't like me.
I love wearing my mother's clothes.

I love a day with no social events.
I love you for reading this poem.

I love the rain.
I love the dark.

I love remembering all who are no longer living.
I love remembering all that I'm living for.

NOTES

The opening quote in this book is borrowed from Jericho Brown's poem "Say Thank You Say I'm Sorry." I also wanted to borrow from Missy Elliot's "4 My People," but it's difficult to get permission to use song lyrics. I'll just say I love you and that song, Missy Elliot, and I'll leave it to everyone's imagination to determine which lines I wanted to quote.

"Poem for the Dead" is styled after Alex Dimitrov's "Poem for the Reader."

"Poem for TOO DARK" is inspired by my Ouija board conversations with a spirit who identifies simply as "TOO DARK." It's also inspired by poets I love who have used Ouija boards to write poems, mainly Sylvia Plath, James Merrill, Lucille Clifton, and Alex Dimitrov.

The line "Can you believe that some of your fans take a trip to Indiana just to see your braid?" in "Poem for Sylvia Plath" was inspired by Diane Seuss' "Self-Portrait with Sylvia Plath's Braid."

"Poem for the Astro Poets" borrows lines from the Astro Poets' Substack post from July 28, 2021, titled "Signs as Punctuation Marks."

"Poem for 17 Mutuals" is a cento, and, in order of appearance, borrows lines from poems in *Emerge Journal* by: Samantha DeFlitch ("Dogs on the Roof," Issue 19); Jared Beloff ("Living Happily at the End of the World," Issue 20); Madeleine Corley ("Theft," Issue 16); Lannie Stabile ("brother, brother, brother," Issue 18); Cyndie Randall ("Your Dreams and Your Light Are Too Ordinary, My Love," Issue 18); Francine Witte ("Why Do You Ask?," Issue 12); Lynne Schmidt ("Learning German," Issue 19); Andrew Bertaina ("In Spain," Issue 20); Aleah Dye ("Body Heat," Issue 15); Rachael Crosbie ("Versions of Fire," Issue 17); C. Cimmone ("Chains," Issue 20); Damian Rucci ("In Places Like This," Issue 16); Ayesha Asad ("Teatime and Boiled Ginger," Issue 13); Lindsey Heatherly ("Routine," Issue 14); Danielle Rose ("Diving," Issue 17); Leigh Chadwick ("Author Writes About Herself in the Third Person or: The Poem of Tiny Clouds," Issue 20); Andrew Bertaina ("In Spain," Issue 20); Marissa Glover ("Homeland," Issue 16). It was previously published in *Emerge*'s 10th Anniversary Issue.

"Poem for the Jurors" is also a semi-cento comprised of lines I heard spoken by various people while seated in the jury waiting room at the Richard E. Gerstein Justice Building in Miami on October 11, 2022. I would cite those people here, but I don't know their names, and I took some liberties with what I heard.

"Poem for People with a Phone in Their Hand" was written in The Writer's Room at The Betsy-South Beach. My thanks to Jonathan Plutzik and Deborah Plutzik

Briggs for lending me their father (Hyam Plutzik)'s desk. This poem is for the three of them and for all who have shared and will share space at that desk.

"Poem for the Living" is styled after Alex Dimitrov's "Love," and an earlier version of this poem appeared in *Something Kindred*, under a different title. If you aren't already, you should follow @apoemcalledlove on Twitter.

ACKNOWLEDGMENTS

Thank you to my one true brother Clifford Brooks III and my family at The Southern Collective Experience Press for publishing this book and believing in me once again. A special shout-out to the amazingly talented Kaitlyn Young for the beautiful cover design, and the equally magical Jackie Taylor for the author headshot.

I am grateful to the editors of the following publications where some of these poems will soon appear or first appeared, at times in earlier versions: *Dreams & Nightmares: An Anthology* (edited by Aura Martin), *FERAL, The Hallowzine, Roi Fainéant Press, THE TICKLE, The Elpis Pages: A Collective* (edited by Kayla King), *SWWIM Every Day, Whale Road Review, HAD, trampset, Maudlin House, Hello, How Can I Help You Today* (edited by Casey Dawson), *Emerge Literary Journal* (10th Anniversary Special Cento Project), *The Alien Buddha's House of Horrors 4* (edited by Red Focks), *It Came From Beneath the Ink! An R.L. Stine Tribute Anthology* (edited by Lannie Stabile), *HELL IS REAL: A Midwest Gothic Anthology* (edited by Jack Hartley), *The Midnight Mass Anthology* (edited by Rachael Crosbie and Charlie D'Aniello), *theVERSEverse, Stone of Madness Press, Limp Wrist,* and *Hello America Stereo Cassette.*

I am grateful to all my poet friends and especially to those who have provided feedback on the poems that make up this manuscript, including the super supportive Jared Beloff, Adrian Dallas Frandle, and Maureen Seaton. My thanks to them, and to Aaron Burch, Michael Chang, Alex Dimitrov, and my dad, Dale Tallman, for the book blurbs.

I am grateful to my partner, Militza, and to my non-poet friends and family who support my art. Thank you, and I love you all.

Most of all, I am grateful to you for reading *Poems for the People*. Thank you so much! These poems are for you. Please continue to read and support contemporary poetry and poets. We can't do this without you.

www.ingramcontent.com/pod-product-compliance
Lightning Source LLC
Chambersburg PA
CBHW072107110526
44590CB00018B/3348